Creature Comparisons

Birds

Tracey Crawford

www.heinemann.co.uk/library
Visit our website to find out more information about **Heinemann Library** books.

To order:
☎ Phone 44 (0) 1865 888066
🖹 Send a fax to 44 (0) 1865 314091
💻 Visit the Heinemann Bookshop at www.heinemann.co.uk/library to browse our catalogue and order online.

First published in Great Britain by Heinemann Library, Halley Court, Jordan Hill, Oxford OX2 8EJ, part of Harcourt Education. Heinemann is a registered trademark of Harcourt Education Ltd.

Editorial: Tracey Crawford, Cassie Mayer, Dan Nunn, and Sarah Chappelow
Design: Jo Hinton-Malivoire
Picture Research: Tracy Cummins and Tracey Engel, and Ruth Blair
Production: Duncan Gilbert

Originated by Chroma Graphics (Overseas) Pte. Ltd
Printed and bound in China by South China Printing Company

10 digit ISBN 0 431 18225 6
13 digit ISBN 978 0 431 18225 4

11 10 09 08 07
10 9 8 7 6 5 4 3 2 1

British Library Cataloguing in Publication Data
Crawford, Tracey
  Birds. - (Creature comparisons)
  1.Birds - Juvenile literature
  I.Title
  598
A full catalogue record for this book is available from the British Library.

Acknowledgements
The publishers would like to thank the following for permission to reproduce photographs: Corbis pp. **4** (monkey, Frank Lukasseck), **5** (Arthur Morris), **6** (W. Perry Conway), **8** (pelican, Theo Allofs), **10** (Farrell Grehan), **11** (Paul A. Souders), **16** (Joe McDonald), **18** (Tom Brakefield), **19** (Arthur Morris), **22** (penguins, Tim Davis; egret, Royalty Free), **23** (seagull eggs, Farrell Grehan; baby birds, Paul A. Souders); Getty Images pp. **4** (fish), **8** (macaw, Digital Vision; eagle, PhotoDisc), **12** (JH Pete Carmichael), **13** (Johnny Johnson), **14** (Don Klumpp), **15** (Roy Toft); NHPA p. **17** (Andy Rouse); Carlton Ward pp. **4** (snake, frog), **7**, **8** (tropical bird), **20**, **21**.

Cover photograph of an emperor penguin reproduced with permission of photolibrary.com/Mark Jones and a blue parrot reproduced with permission of Corbis/Royalty Free.

Every effort has been made to contact copyright holders of any material reproduced in this book. Any omissions will be rectified in subsequent printings if notice is given to the publishers.

Contents

There are many types of animals.

Birds are one type of animal.

All birds have feathers.

All birds have two wings.

All birds have a beak.

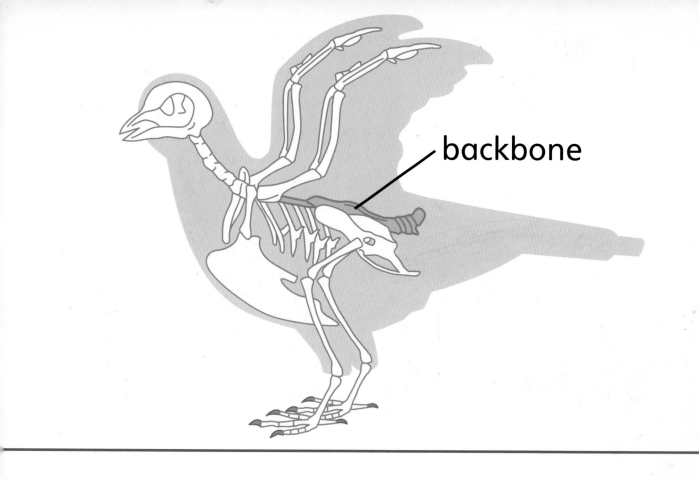

backbone

All birds have a backbone.

egg

All baby birds hatch from an egg.

nest

All baby birds live in a nest.

Most birds can fly.

But these birds cannot fly.

Some birds are big.

Some birds are small.

Some birds fly high.

Some birds fly low.

Some birds swim.

Some birds dive.

Every bird is different.

Every bird is special.

Bird facts

Birds that can fly have very light bones. This helps them fly.

Penguins use their wings like paddles. This helps them swim.

Picture glossary

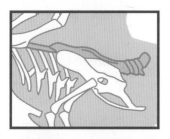 **backbone** the part of the skeleton that goes from the head to the tail

 **hatch** to be born from an egg

 **nest** the home where a baby bird is born

Index

Notes to parents and teachers
Before reading
Talk to the children about birds. Does anyone keep a pet bird? What different birds can they name?

After reading
Sing the nursery rhyme: "Two little dicky birds sitting on a wall. One named Peter, the other named Paul. Fly away Peter. Fly away Paul. Come back Peter. Come back Paul." Show children the hand actions to go with the rhyme, using a thumb for each of the birds which fly behind the children's backs.
Make a pine cone bird feeder: Tie a long piece of thin string to the top of the cone. Mix together some lard and plenty of porridge oats. Add some sunflower seeds and chopped dried fruit. Roll the pine cone in the mixture. Hang the bird feeder outside.
Make a CD bird: Make tail feathers from strips of brightly coloured paper and tape them to an unwanted CD. Make two wings from coloured paper and tape these on either side of the CD. Use a "V"-shaped piece of yellow card for the beak. Cut a small opening in the back of the beak and fix on the edge of the CD. Put two dots for eyes on the CD. Suspend the "birds" from the ceiling.

24

Titles in the *Creature Comparisons* series include:

Hardback   0 431 18226 4

Hardback   0 431 18225 6

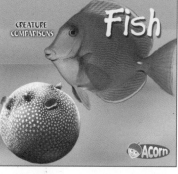

Hardback   0 431 18224 8

Hardback   0 431 18228 0

Hardback   0 431 18223 X

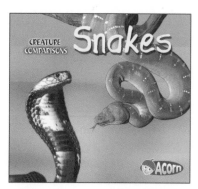

Hardback   0 431 18227 2

Find out about other titles from Heinemann Library on our website www.heinemann.co.uk/library